Mammals

Sally Morgan

Raintree

Chicago, Illinois

© 2005 Raintree
Published by Raintree, a division of Reed Elsevier Inc.
Chicago, Illinois
Customer Service 888-363-4266
Visit our website at www.raintreelibrary.com

For information, address the publisher:
Raintree, 100 N. LaSalle, Suite 1200, Chicago, IL 60602

Produced for Raintree by
White-Thomson Publishing Ltd.

Consultant: Dr. Rod Preston-Mafham
Page layout by Tim Mayer
Photo research by Sally Morgan

Originated by Dot Gradations Ltd.
Printed in China by WKT Company Limited

09 08 07 06 05
10 9 8 7 6 5 4 3 2 1

Library of Congress Cataloging-in-Publication Data
Morgan, Sally.
  Mammals / Sally Morgan.
    p. cm. -- (Animal kingdom)
Includes bibliographical references (p.   ) and index.
Contents: Mammals -- Feeding -- Communicating -- The
carnivores -- The
primates -- The rodents -- The minor orders.
  ISBN 1-4109-1050-4 (library binding : hardcover) --
ISBN 1-4109-1346-5 (pbk.)
  1. Mammals--Juvenile literature. [1. Mammals.] I. Title. II.
Series:
Morgan, Sally   Animal kingdom.
  QL706.2.M55 2005
  599--dc22
                                        2003024892

Acknowledgments
The publisher would like to thank the following for permission to
reproduce copyright materials: Corbis **Title page**, **60** bottom;
Digital Stock pp.**10**, **16**, **33** top, **38**; Digital Vision pp.**4**, **8**, **13**
top, **15** top left, **29** bottom, **31** top, **35**, **51**, **58**, **60** top;
Ecoscene pp.**9** bottom (Fritz Pölking), **11** top (Christine
Osborne), **17** top (Fritz Pölking), **19** (Brandon Cole / V&W), **24**
top (Fritz Pölking), **26** top and **27** top (S. Tiwari), **28** (Karl
Ammann), **30** (Fritz Pölking), **39** top (Robin Redfern), **42**
(Philip Colla), **43** top and bottom, and **44** bottom left (Brandon
Cole / V&W), **44** main, **45**, and **46** (Philip Colla), **47** bottom
(Brandon Cole / V&W), **49** middle (Michael Gore), **55** top
(Robert Baldwin), **55** bottom (Tom Ennis), **56** (Pete Cairns), **57**
top (Fritz Pölking), **59** (Philip Colla); Ecoscene – Papilio pp.**13**
bottom (Dennis Johnson), **48** bottom and **49** top (Robert
Pickett); Nature Picture Library pp.**9** top (George McCarthy), **15**
bottom and **21** bottom (Anup Shah), **24** bottom (Bruce
Davidson), **25** main (Brian Lightfoot), **26** main (Anup Shah), **31**
bottom (Bruce Davidson), **34** top (T.J. Rich), **36** (Richard Du
Toit), **39** bottom (Peter Blackwell), **47** top (Aflo), **50** left (Ingo
Arndt), **57** bottom (Staffan Widstrand); NHPA pp.**5** bottom right
(Martin Harvey), **6** and **7** (Jonathan and Angela Scott), **7** top
(Laurie Campbell), **7** bottom (Martin Harvey), **11** bottom (Joe
Blossom), **12** (Martin Harvey), **14** (ANT), **17** bottom
(Christophe Ratier), **18** top (Kevin Schafer), **18** bottom (Nick
Garbutt), **20** (Mike Lane), **21** top (Jonathan and Angela Scott),
22–**23** and **23** bottom (Nigel Dennis), **23** top (G.I. Bernard), **29**
top (Martin Harvey), **32** top (Laurie Campbell), **32** bottom
(Daryl Balfour), **34** bottom (Martin Harvey), **37** top right
(Anthony Bannister), **40** top (Daniel Heuclin), **40** bottom (Guy
Edwardes), **41** (Michael Leach), **50** right and **52** top (ANT), **52**
bottom (Daniel Heuclin), **53** (Dave Watts), **54**–**55** (T. Kitchen
and V. Hirst); Photodisc pp. **5** top right, **37** bottom left.

Front cover photograph of zebra reproduced with permission of
NHPA (Kevin Schafer). Back cover photograph of a zebra
reproduced with permission of Ecoscene (Sally Morgan).

Every effort has been made to contact copyright holders of any
material reproduced in this book. Any omissions will be rectified
in subsequent printings if notice is given to the publisher.

Contents

Introducing Mammals

Mammals are found almost everywhere in the world, from the tropical rain forests to the frozen poles, on land, in the air, and in water. There are more than 4,600 different types of mammals. Mammals are the only animals that have hair and feed their young milk.

Mammals belong to a large group of animals called vertebrates. These are animals with backbones. The backbone is made up of small bones hinged together and the spinal cord, a group of nerves running through the middle. Other vertebrates include fish, amphibians, reptiles, and birds.

Teeth, ears, and hair

Adult mammals usually have four types of teeth: incisors, canines, premolars, and molars. The teeth are adapted to suit the diet of the mammal. Mammals also usually have an outer ear, or pinna, on the outside of their heads to funnel sounds into the inner ear.

Only mammals have true hair, which grows continuously from the root. Hair is made of a substance called keratin. Hair can be thick, forming fur, or as sparse as it is on the human body.

Whiskers, spines, and some horns are made of modified hair. Some mammals, such as hippos and whales, have lost their hair as an adaptation to their environments.

Classification key

KINGDOM	Animalia
PHYLUM	Chordata
SUB-PHYLUM	Vertebrata
CLASS	**Mammalia**

▶ Brown bears have thick fur to trap heat and keep them warm.

Adaptable animals

Mammals are highly adaptable and are able to change their behavior to suit their environment. One feature that makes mammals adaptable is their ability to maintain a constant body temperature, regardless of the temperature of their surroundings. This feature is called endothermy. For example, a polar bear's thick fur and fat layers trap heat so it can keep its body temperature at around 98° Fahrenheit (37° Celsius) even when the outside temperature may be below freezing. Mammals are not the only endothermic animals. Birds can regulate their body temperatures, too. Other animals, such as reptiles, have a body temperature that changes with their surroundings, and they become inactive at low temperatures.

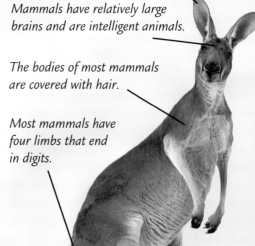

The outer ear funnels sound into the inner ear, which is within the skull.

Mammals have relatively large brains and are intelligent animals.

The bodies of most mammals are covered with hair.

Most mammals have four limbs that end in digits.

▶ Mammals share many similar characteristics.

◀ Female mammals feed their young with milk from special glands called mammary glands. It is from these glands that mammals get their name.

Classification

Living organisms are classified, or organized, according to how closely related one organism is to another. A species is a group of individuals that are similar to each other and that can interbreed with one another. Species are grouped together into genera. A single genus may contain species that share some features. Genera are grouped together in families, the families grouped into orders, and the orders grouped into classes. Mammals belong to the class Mammalia. Classes are grouped together in a phylum, and finally the phyla are grouped into kingdoms. Kingdoms are the largest groups. Mammals belong to the animal kingdom.

Mammal Behavior and Life Cycle

Most mammals give birth to live young. It is this feature of mammals that makes them different from other animals. Mammals can be divided into three groups: monotremes, marsupials, and placental mammals.

Monotremes such as the platypus are primitive mammals that lay eggs. Both marsupials and placental mammals give birth to live young. However, marsupials give birth to young at a very early stage of development. These marsupial babies are tiny, blind, deaf, and hairless. They use their front legs to clamber through their mother's fur to her pouch, where they spend many months drinking her milk.

Placental mammals such as the horse give birth to well-developed young. The young mammal does a lot of growing while it is still inside its mother. It grows inside the uterus, or womb. On one side of the uterus is an organ called the placenta. Oxygen and food pass through the placenta from the mother's blood into the blood supply of the unborn baby. Carbon dioxide and other waste passes back to the mother's blood.

▶ Lions are placental mammals. They live for about fifteen years in the wild.

The length of time between the fertilization of the egg and birth is called the gestation period. In small mammals such as mice and rats, the gestation period is just a few weeks. The babies are born hairless and helpless. Gestation is much longer in larger mammals. The gestation period of a human being is nine months.

Parental care

Female mammals feed their babies milk they produce in their mammary glands. The milk contains all the nutrition the baby needs. The babies are fed milk until their teeth develop and they can chew adult food. The change from milk to solid food is called weaning. Some mammals spend years looking after their young. Other mammals produce young that can live independently within a few weeks.

Life span

In general, the larger the mammal, the longer its life span. The longest-lived mammals include human beings, elephants, and whales. Some of the smallest mammals, such as shrews, have very short life spans. They grow quickly and live for only a year or two.

▲ This guanaco is giving birth to her young. The newborn guanaco will be able to run around within minutes of birth.

▼ Mammals such as this ring-tailed lemur care for young until they are able to look after themselves.

Amazing facts

○ The female lemming gives birth sixteen days after mating and can produce up to twelve babies. Each baby is ready to mate at three weeks of age!

○ A male marsupial called the brown antechinus lives for just a few months. He fathers only one litter and does not live long enough to see the birth of his offspring.

Staying Warm

Imagine living in a place where the temperatures can fall to -49° Fahrenheit (-45° Celsius). Amazingly, some mammals, such as the polar bear and the Arctic fox, can survive these temperatures. Mammals can keep their body temperature almost constant even though the temperature of their surroundings may change. They have various ways of keeping their temperature within a narrow range. If their body temperature falls, mammals may shiver or their hair may stand up on end to trap heat. Mammals also move around to generate heat. If the temperature rises, mammals lose heat by sweating or panting. However, for mammals that live in permanently cold climates, these methods are not enough. Their bodies have adapted, or changed, to cope with the climate.

Fur and fat

Polar mammals cannot afford to lose body heat, so good insulation is essential. The bodies of polar mammals are covered in a layer of fat called blubber and thick fur. Blubber is so good at trapping heat that the skin above it may feel cold to the touch even though the mammal is perfectly warm inside.

▲ Sea lions have a thick layer of blubber and waterproof fur.

Hibernation

During winter, many small mammals hibernate, or go into a deep sleep. Their small size and large surface area means they have to eat a lot of food each day just to keep warm. Food can be scarce during winter so many small mammals survive by hibernating. During the autumn, they put on layers of fat and then creep into a nest to sleep. Their hearts beat slowly, and their body temperature falls to just above that of their surroundings. Hibernating mammals survive by using up fat reserves. They stay in hibernation until the outside temperatures rise again and more food becomes available.

▲ This dormouse looks as if it is asleep, but it is actually hibernating.

Amazing facts

- The Arctic fox is so well insulated that it can sleep on the snow at temperatures of -116° Fahrenheit (-80° Celsius) for up to an hour.
- A polar bear can easily overheat if it runs too fast. It may eat snow or lie flat on the ice to cool off.

▼ A polar bear may look white, but underneath its fur its skin is black. Dark skin absorbs more heat than light skin does.

Surviving in the Desert

Desert mammals have adapted to survive extreme temperatures. In the desert, daytime temperatures can soar to 122° Fahrenheit (50° Celsius). This is dangerous because if a mammal's body temperature rises by just a few degrees, it may die from heat stroke. At night, however, the desert can be very cold and the mammal has to keep warm.

Keeping cool

To cool down, mammals sweat or pant. Sweat glands in the skin produce a watery liquid that evaporates, cooling the skin. Not all mammals sweat. Dogs, for example, cool off by panting. They open their mouths and hang out their tongues to increase the surface area from which water can evaporate. Many mammals avoid the hot sun by hiding in the shade in underground burrows until nightfall, when it is cooler.

A few mammals can actually trick their brains into thinking they are cooler than they really are. Normally, cooling processes start to work when a mammal's body reaches a certain temperature. The blood of the desert oryx cools as it flows through the animal's nose. This cooled blood goes to the animal's brain and the brain thinks the temperature is acceptable. This means that valuable water is not lost in sweating and panting.

◄ A desert oryx can walk for hours to find food. During the hottest hours of the day, an oryx will rest under shady trees.

▲ A camel's hump is full of fat, which it uses as fuel when there is no food around.

Amazing camel facts

- Camels have long eyelashes and slitlike nostrils that can close during sandstorms.
- Camels' thick fur insulates against the heat during the day and prevents heat loss at night.
- Adult camels can drink as much as 35 gallons (136 liters) of water within a very short period of time.

Finding water

To survive, desert mammals have to be able to find enough water. Many rely on the water in the plants that they eat. They eat fleshy fruits and leaves full of water. Some mammals can get enough water from eating seeds and never drink water at all.

Body shape

The bodies of desert mammals tend to be shaped to lose heat rather than conserve it. For example, they are often slim, long-legged animals. This creates a large surface area over which heat can be lost. Blood flows close to the surface of the skin to lose heat. Some large mammals, such as elephants, rhinos, and hippos, live in hot climates. They have difficulty cooling off because the center of their bodies is a long way from the surface. They do not have hair, so heat can escape more easily from the surface of the skin. Elephants have large ears and can keep cool by flapping them.

▶ Fennec foxes hunt at night when it is cooler. Their long ears enable them to hear their prey moving around in the dark.

11

Feeding

Mammals feed in many different ways. What a mammal eats dictates the shape of its jaw and the arrangement of its teeth. Adult mammals have four different kinds of teeth—incisors, canines, premolars, and molars.

Carnivores, or meat eaters, have long, curved canines for stabbing and killing their prey. Rodents have large incisors for gnawing. Herbivores, or plant eaters, have large, ridged molars that are ideal for grinding plant food.

Termite eaters

Each day, giant anteaters, armadillos, and pangolins feed on thousands of ants and termites. Their long, curved claws are ideal for ripping open termite nests. These animals also have long tongues that are covered in gluey saliva so that the termites stick to them. The bodies of armadillos and pangolins are covered in tough scales that act like a coat of armor. When hundreds of angry termites swarm out to protect their nest, these mammals simply press their scales firmly together, close their eyelids and nostrils, and keep on eating!

Amazing facts

- The aye-aye, a type of lemur, has a long, thin middle finger that ends in a claw. It uses this finger to pull out larvae from holes in trees.
- The vampire bat feeds on blood from other mammals. It uses its incisors to carefully shave hair from a patch of skin and cut two grooves in it. The bat then laps up the blood that oozes from the cut.
- The giant armadillo is the mammal with the most teeth. It has about 100!

◀ Chimpanzees have hands that can grip food and use tools, such as this twig, to reach termites.

Tool users

Chimpanzees have hands similar to human beings, with a thumb that lies at a right angle to the fingers. This means that they can grip and manipulate objects. Chimpanzees have learned to use tools to help them find food. For example, a chimpanzee will poke a stick into a termites' nest. The chimpanzee pulls the stick out and licks off the termites.

Herbivores

The savannas of southern Africa are home to many different types of herbivores. Many feed on grass, but others eat the leaves of the trees and shrubs. Although there are large numbers of herbivores, they do not always compete with each other for food. For example, several different types of herbivores feed on the leaves of the acacia tree. Small antelopes and impalas eat leaves from the lower branches while the gerenuk stands on its back legs to reach the higher leaves. The giraffe, the tallest of all the mammals, browses on leaves near the top of the tree.

▶ A long neck allows giraffes to reach the higher leaves that other animals cannot reach.

Mammal Movement

Mammals get around by walking, running, jumping, flying, or swimming. Most mammals have four limbs, but in some mammals the limbs have adapted for a particular type of movement.

Hoofs for running

Hoofed mammals, such as zebras and antelopes, have long legs for running great distances. The longer their legs, the quicker an animal can run. Hoofed mammals must be able to outrun their predators. These predators have adapted to be able to run fast over short distances and are equipped with powerful muscles.

Flight

The only animals that can fly are birds, insects, and bats. Bats are mammals with arms that form wings for flying. A bat's wing is like a thin sheet formed from a double layer of skin. It stretches from the legs and the sides of the body to the fingers. Bats have four long fingers to support their wings.

▼ Bats are nocturnal and fly at night. This Australian ghost bat has a wingspan of about 20 inches (50 cm). It hunts large insects, reptiles, frogs, birds, and small mammals.

Swinging through trees

Mammals that live in trees usually have long limbs that they use to climb and swing through the branches. Gibbons, a type of ape, live their entire lives in the trees. They have very long arms that they use to swing from branch to branch. They do not have tails. Gibbons, which have been described as the acrobats of the mammal world, can move quickly through the trees.

Swimming

Marine mammals, such as whales, dolphins, and seals, live in water and their bodies are adapted to swimming. These mammals have a streamlined shape that tapers to the tail. It is important to have a smooth outline to slip through the water easily. Whales and dolphins do not have any hair on their skin, and this creates an even smoother surface. Marine mammals use rounded, paddle-like limbs called flippers to steer. The whale has a huge tail fin that it uses to push itself through the water.

▲ The gibbon moves with ease through the trees, swinging from branch to branch. This method of movement is called brachiation.

Amazing facts

- The large mouse-eared bat has a wingspan of up to 19 inches (38 centimeters). It travels 125 miles (200 kilometers) across Europe between its winter and summer feeding places.

- The colugo, or flying lemur, can glide over distances of up to 447 feet (136 meters). It has a huge membrane stretched between its arms, legs, and head to form what looks like a wing. However, the colugo's wing is so large that the animal can hardly move on the ground.

- Male western gray kangaroos can travel more than 33 feet (10 meters) in a single leap.

▲ Hoofed feet allow the warthog to move quickly over hard ground.

The Cheetah

The cheetah, which can run at speeds of 62 miles per hour, is the fastest land animal. Like a sports car, the cheetah can go from a dead stop to its top speed in just a few seconds. This means the cheetah is able to outrun all other animals over a short distance. However, the cheetah can keep up these amazing speeds for only up to 20 seconds before its body overheats and it has to slow down. If a cheetah's prey can stay ahead long enough, it will escape.

Getting close

Since cheetahs can run fast for a only few hundred feet, they must get very close to their prey before starting their chase. Cheetahs creep up on their prey until they are about 30 meters away by moving low in the grass and approaching from downwind. This may take just a few seconds or as long as several hours. Unlike many other carnivores, cheetahs hunt during the day because they need to be able to see their prey.

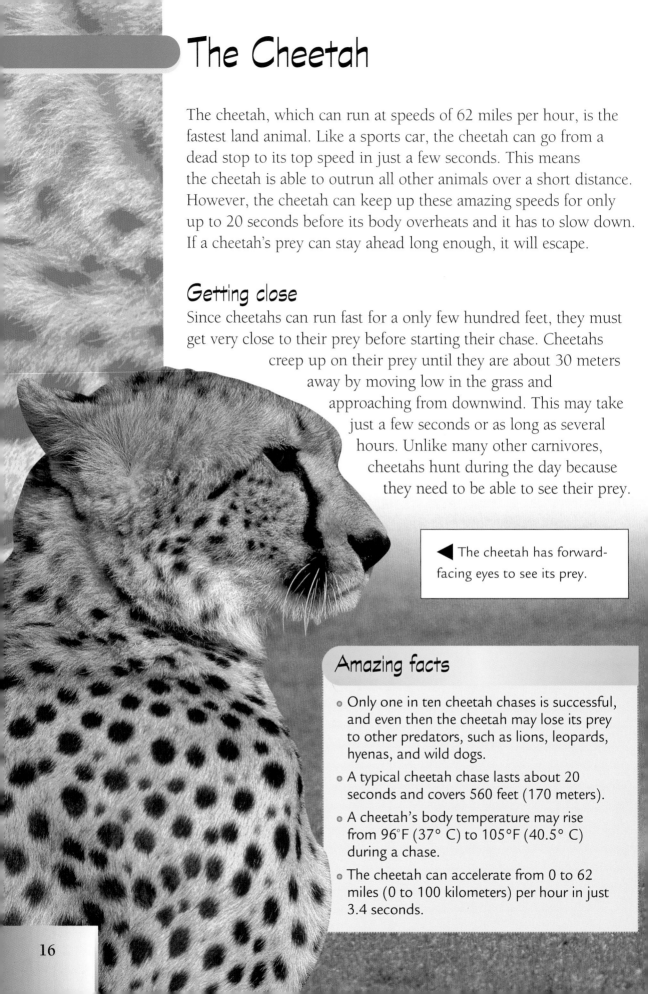

◀ The cheetah has forward-facing eyes to see its prey.

Amazing facts

- Only one in ten cheetah chases is successful, and even then the cheetah may lose its prey to other predators, such as lions, leopards, hyenas, and wild dogs.
- A typical cheetah chase lasts about 20 seconds and covers 560 feet (170 meters).
- A cheetah's body temperature may rise from 96°F (37° C) to 105°F (40.5° C) during a chase.
- The cheetah can accelerate from 0 to 62 miles (0 to 100 kilometers) per hour in just 3.4 seconds.

The chase

The cheetah gets its speed in part from its extremely flexible skeleton. It allows the animal's backbone to curve up and down, giving the animal a long stride. The cheetah may be able to run very fast in a straight line, but it has to be able to make turns, too, because its prey will dart and dodge to try to escape. The cheetah has claws that stick out to provide grip during high-speed turns. The cheetah's tail has a flat surface, like the rudder of a boat, which helps it to balance its body as it runs. Stopping presents another problem. When the cheetah tackles its prey, it is moving at full speed. The cheetah has to be able to stop quickly. The cheetah stops by slamming down its two front legs, which act like brakes on a car. Pointed pads on the back of the front legs tear into the ground, bringing the cheetah to an almost immediate halt. Then, the cheetah grabs its prey before it can escape. The cheetah suffocates the prey by biting the underside of the its throat. The prey is dragged away to shelter and eaten.

▼ This group of young cheetahs is learning how to hunt.

Classification key

ORDER	Carnivora
FAMILY	Felidae
GENUS	*Acinomyx*
SPECIES	***Acinomyx jubatus***

◄ The cheetah uses its tail to balance while running.

Communicating

▲ The howl of the male howler monkey carries far. The howls help different groups of monkeys, called troops, keep in contact with each other in the forest.

Mammals use their well-developed senses of sight, hearing, touch, smell, and taste to communicate with each other and to explore their surroundings.

Importance of color

Primates are the only mammals that can see in full color. Rain forests are dark places where brown or black animals are hard to see, so some monkeys use color to communicate. Color helps the different species identify one another. For example, mandrills have a bright-colored face with a red nose and blue cheeks, while the uakari has a bald red head and face.

Sound and smell

Many mammals live in specific areas, called territories, which they defend against intruders. Sound is an important tool for telling would-be intruders that the territory has an owner. Examples are the roaring of lions and tigers. Some mammals mark the boundaries of their territory with scent. These mammals have scent-producing glands around their face, feet, or under their tails. Hyenas and lions use urine as a scent marker. They mark stones and trees along the edges of their territory where the scent can be detected by others.

▼ A tiger sprays urine against a tree at nose height so that its scent can be detected easily by other tigers.

Echolocation and sonar

Some mammals use sound to help them find their way around.
Bats, for example, use a special system called echolocation. A bat
produces high-pitched sounds in its voice box, or larynx, which are
emitted through the nose or mouth. These sounds bounce off objects
in front of the bat. The bat's specialized ears pick up the returning
echoes, which tell the bat about the position of objects in its path.

▼ Dolphins communicate
using chirping, whistling, and
squeaking sounds.

Amazing facts

○ A dolphin can emit as many
as 2,000 clicks per second.

○ Bush babies urinate on their
hands and feet so that when
they climb around the forest
they leave behind a trail
of scent.

○ White rhinos stamp in their
dung to spread their own
smell with each step.

Dolphins also use sound to help detect prey
while swimming. This is a type of sonar, similar
to that used by submarines. The dolphin
produces a series of low- and high-pitched clicks.
When any of these clicks hit an object, the sound
waves they produce bounce back to the dolphin. The high-pitched clicks
provide information about close objects, such as the size and type of a
nearby fish. Low-pitched clicks travel further and help a dolphin locate
and identify objects that are further away.

Living Together

While some mammals live alone, a few live with a partner and many live together in groups. Mammal groups may stay together permanently or just for short periods of time. Some groups consist only of males or all females while other groups include both sexes. Mammals that live on their own, such as aardvarks, usually meet up with others only to mate. Gibbons live in pairs and look after their young until they can survive on their own.

Living in groups

There are advantages to living in groups, especially for the smaller mammals. Predators are easier to spot, so there is a greater chance of escape. Living in a group also makes it easier to protect a territory against intruders. Some mammals help each other raise young so that more survive and grow to adulthood. For example, meerkats live in groups of up to 30 animals. One or two meerkats climb up on mounds or bushes to watch for predators while the others feed. They gang up to chase away some predators.

Amazing facts

- Prairie dogs live in huge underground burrows called cities. One of the largest cities found was in Texas. It covered 24,500 square miles and was believed to be home to 400 million prairie dogs.

- In Australia, fruit bats known as flying foxes roost together in trees. Up to 1 million may live in a single group.

▲ When a troop of monkeys rests during the day, the animals often spend time grooming each other.

A pride of lions

Lions live in groups called prides that consist of up to twelve lionesses, their young, and up to six males. Each pride lives in a territory that individuals defend against other prides. There are many advantages to living in a pride. Hunting is more successful when it involves teamwork. Lions working together can also more easily steal prey from other carnivores and protect their own kills from hyenas.

▲ Lionesses and their cubs watch over the savanna.

Elephant herds

Female elephants live with their offspring in a group called a herd. The herd is led by the oldest female, or matriarch. Female elephants that have reached adulthood stay with the herd. However, the males leave to either live alone or travel with other young males. Elephants are long lived, and the matriarch may lead her herd for many years. The herd benefits from her experience in finding food and water and avoiding danger.

▼ Like elephants, wildebeests live in herds. This herd of wildebeests is crossing a river in search of fresh grazing areas.

21

Mammalian Orders

The class of mammals is divided into smaller groups called subclasses. There are three subclasses of mammals: monotremes (Prototheria), marsupials (Theria), and placental mammals (Eutheria). The monotremes and marsupials are the two primitive groups that include 297 species in total. By far the largest subclass is the placental mammals, which consist of about 4,330 species. The subclasses are further divided into groups called orders. There are 21 different mammalian orders. Scientists called biologists study the features of the different mammals and place those with similar features into the same order.

▶ Meerkats are carnivores. They live in burrows under the ground and emerge each morning to hunt for prey.

Amazing facts

- The world's smallest mammal is Kitti's hog-nosed bat, *Craseonycteris thonglongyai*, from Thailand. It is just a little over an inch (3 cm) long and weighs less than .06 lb (2 g), which makes it smaller than many insects and snails.

- The largest land animal is the bull, or male, African elephant. The largest specimen recorded stood around 52 ft (3.96 m) tall at the shoulder and weighed more than 13 tons (12 metric tons).

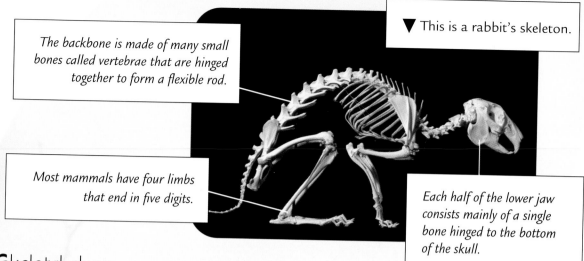

The backbone is made of many small bones called vertebrae that are hinged together to form a flexible rod.

▼ This is a rabbit's skeleton.

Most mammals have four limbs that end in five digits.

Each half of the lower jaw consists mainly of a single bone hinged to the bottom of the skull.

Skeletal clues

To divide the placental mammals into different orders, it is necessary to look at features such as their skeletons. Primates and insectivores have four limbs that end in five fingers or toes. In some orders, the limb has changed, or evolved, into a different shape. In the bat, the front limb has four long fingers to support its wings. Whales and dolphins have short front limbs and the digits form a flipper for swimming. They have lost their hind limbs. Some mammals have long legs that end in hooves. Hoofed mammals can be separated into two orders: those with an even number of toes such as deer (Artiodactyla), and those with an odd number such as zebras (Perissodactyla).

The skull

The skull of placental mammals is made up of about 34 bones that are fused together. There are three parts: the cranium, which encloses the brain, the rostrum (snout and upper jaw), and the lower jaw. The lower jaw consists of just a single bone on either side that attach to the bottom of the cranium. A mammal's skull provides clues about its diet. Carnivores have forward-facing eye sockets that enable them to judge distances and spot prey. They have sharp, pointed canine teeth that are long and curved for stabbing. The skull of a herbivore has teeth that are adapted to tear up and chew plants and large, sideways-facing eye sockets for a wide field of vision.

▼ Pangolins belong to the order Pholidota. They are covered in scales which give protection and camouflage.

Carnivores

▼ Large, sharp teeth allow these polar bears to tear up their prey.

Carnivores, the hunters of the mammal world, prey on other animals. They vary in size, ranging from the large Kodiak bear (a type of brown bear) to the tiny weasel. Carnivores can be found in many different climates around the world. Polar bears and Arctic foxes are found in the Arctic, and there are carnivores, such as jaguars and wolves, in rain forests and deserts.

Teeth for stabbing

The teeth of carnivores are adapted to their meat diet. Carnivores use their teeth to grip, kill, and then eat their prey. They have four long, curved canine teeth—two on the top jaw and two on the bottom jaw. Canine teeth are used to stab and hold on to prey. In the back of their mouths, canines have four large teeth known as the carnassials. These teeth are razor sharp and can slice through skin and muscle. Carnivores have powerful jaw muscles essential for capturing and tearing up prey.

▼ African prairie dogs hunt in groups called packs. They hunt impalas, antelopes, wildebeests, and gazelles, usually targeting the youngest or weakest animals in a herd.

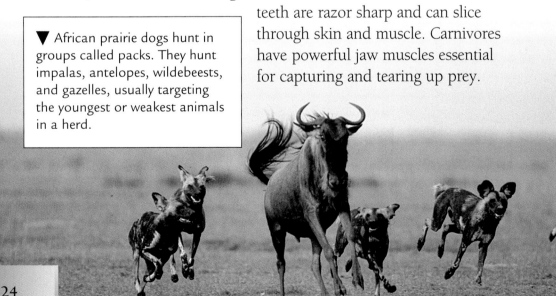

Catching prey

Carnivores find their prey using well-developed senses of sight, hearing, and smell. Many carnivores creep up on their prey and pounce when they are close. Some, such as the African wild dog or the cheetah, chase their prey. These carnivores have a flexible spine and long legs. Larger hunters, such as lions and tigers, have powerful shoulders that they use to pull down their prey, which is often much larger than themselves. Some carnivores kill their prey by biting through its neck or skull, while others suffocate their victims. Some carnivores, such as the wolf or the lion, hunt in groups to improve their chances of success.

Amazing facts

- The giant panda is a carnivore that eats a few insects but feeds mainly on bamboo shoots and roots.
- The sharp teeth and the strong jaw muscles of the spotted hyena enable it to crush bones and rip through skin and tendons too tough for other carnivores to eat.
- The Kodiak bear is the world's largest land carnivore, weighing nearly half a ton. Despite its size, it can charge at speeds of up to 30 miles (50 kilometers) per hour.

Classification key

SUBCLASS	Eutheria
ORDER	**Carnivora**
FAMILIES	7 (Cat, dog, bear, raccoon, weasel, civet, and hyena)
SPECIES	249

▲ The stoat may be a smaller carnivore, but it can kill prey as large as rabbits.

The Tiger

The tiger is the largest of all the cats. It is a powerful animal with a muscular body, a large head, and long canine teeth for stabbing prey. Tigers are found across central Asia, including China, India, Malaysia, and Indonesia.

▲ Tigers may be large, but they are agile, too. They can jump and swim and have been known to climb trees.

Tiger basics

Tigers live alone in their own territories. The size of a tiger's territory depends on its habitat and the number of prey animals available. Tigers are superb hunters that prey on large mammals such as wild boars, deer, and even elephants. They hunt at night when prey animals are most active. The tiger creeps up on its prey either from the side or from behind. It gets as close as possible before pouncing. The tiger grabs the prey using its teeth and claws. The weight of the tiger's body brings its victim crashing to the ground. Then the tiger quickly grips its prey by the neck, blocking its windpipe and suffocating it. The tiger bites through the neck of smaller prey.

Classification key

SUBCLASS	Eutheria
ORDER	Carnivora
FAMILY	Felidae
GENUS	*Panthera*
SPECIES	***Panthera tigris***
SUBSPECIES	5 (see fact box on page 27)

Female tigers give birth to as many as 3 cubs. Tiger cubs are born blind and weigh only about 2 lbs (1 kg). They live on their mother's milk for 6 to 8 weeks before they follow her on hunts and start to eat meat. Tiger cubs begin making their own kills when they are about 18 months old. By the time they are 2 years old, young tigers are ready to leave their mother.

▲ Once a tiger has made a kill, it takes its prey to a shelter where it can eat.

Tigers under threat

Today, tigers are endangered mammals. There are barely 7,000 tigers left in the wild. The number of tigers has fallen rapidly for various reasons. Their forest habitat has been cleared for farmland, timber, and industry. Many tigers are killed because people are scared of them. Farmers shoot them to protect their livestock. One of the major threats comes from poaching. People kill tigers for their skin and bones, which are used in traditional Chinese medicines.

▼ These tiger cubs will stay with their mother until they are two years old, when they will be powerful enough to hunt on their own.

Amazing facts – tiger subspecies

- Bengal—found in Indian forests and swamps, weighs up to 570 lbs (260 kg); up to 4,700 left in the wild.
- Sumatran—the smallest tiger, found in forests of Sumatra, Indonesia; fewer than 500 in the wild.
- Indochinese—found in Southeast Asia; up to 1,500 left in the wild.
- Siberian—the biggest cat, weighing up to 770 lbs (350 kg); no more than 400 left in the wild and just under 500 in zoos.
- South China—the rarest tiger, weighing just 330 lbs (150 kg); there are fewer than 30 in the wild and 50 in zoos.

Primates

Primates are among the most familiar mammals because they include human beings, or *Homo sapiens*. Primates have much larger brains than other mammals in proportion to their body size. Human beings have the largest brains of all the mammals. The order is divided up into two suborders—the primitive prosimians and the more advanced anthropoids (monkeys and apes).

▲ Many primates live in Southeast Asia, including apes such as orangutans.

Grasping hands and feet

Most primates have fingers and toes that end in flat nails rather than claws. The apes' big toes and thumbs are opposable, which means they can grasp objects. Sensitive pads on the underside of the fingers and toes help primates grip. Human beings do not have the opposable big toe. Our thumbs are opposable, and can be rotated into a position opposite our fingers to give a powerful grip.

Classification key

SUBCLASS	Eutheria
ORDER	**Primate**
FAMILIES	11
SPECIES	356

Amazing facts

- The smallest primate is the pygmy mouse lemur, which weighs around 30 grams.
- The largest primate is the gorilla, which can weigh up to 200 kilograms.
- In the forests of western Africa, groups of chimpanzees work together to chase and kill monkeys for food.

Prosimians

Prosimians include lemurs, lorises, and galagos. Prosimians are found mostly in forests. They are often nocturnal and have large, round eyes and good night vision. Prosimians have an unusual arrangement of teeth on the lower jaw, where four to six teeth are pressed together to form a sort of dental comb used for grooming.

Monkeys and apes

Monkeys are forest-dwelling primates, too. They move around the trees by running and leaping between branches. Monkeys have short, flat faces, flexible spines, and flattened chests. Their legs are longer than their arms and they walk on all fours, using their tails for balance. Some monkey species have a prehensile tail that acts like a fifth limb. The prehensile tail has muscles and can curl around branches, helping the monkey move through the trees.

Apes include gibbons, orangutans, chimpanzees, gorillas, and human beings. Apes have a shorter spine than monkeys do and broad hips that give a more upright posture. Apes have broad chests and shoulder joints allowing a wide range of movements. Apes have prominent lower jaws and flatter faces than monkeys do.

▲ Lemurs, like all primates, have forward-facing eyes that help them to judge distances as they travel from one place to another.

▼ The hands and feet of primates are described as dextrous, which means that they can handle objects easily.

29

The Gorilla

The gorilla is one of humans' closest relatives. It is the largest of the primates, reaching a height of just under 6 ft (2 m) and weighing up to 440 lbs (200 kg). Gorillas walk on all fours, on the soles of their hind feet, and on the knuckles of their hands.

There are two species of gorilla. The western gorilla is found in western and central Africa. About 100,000 still remain in tropical forests. The eastern gorilla is found in central and eastern Africa. There are three subspecies of gorilla, the best known of which is the mountain gorilla. This gorilla has long, shaggy fur that keeps it warm high up in the mountains.

Classification key

SUBCLASS	Eutheria
ORDER	Primate
FAMILY	Pongidae
GENUS	*Gorilla*
SPECIES	*Gorilla gorilla* (western gorilla) and *Gorilla beringei* (eastern gorilla)

Family groups

Gorillas live in family groups. A typical group of mountain gorillas is made up of one or two adult males aged twelve years or older (called silverbacks), several young males (blackbacks), and a number of females, juveniles, and infants. One of the oldest males in the group, the dominant male, leads the group in its search for food and protects them from such dangers as other males. The dominant male will father most of the offspring in the group.

◀ When gorillas feel threatened, they make loud sounds, such as roars and screams. They use facial expressions to communicate, too.

◀ An adult male gorilla is much larger than a female. He has a bony crest above his head and a band of silver fur across his back.

Gorilla females do not mate until they are about ten years old. They usually give birth to one baby, which they carry around for up to eight months. A female gorilla holds her newborn offspring close to her chest at first, but soon the infant learns how to hold on for itself. It rides on its mother's back until it is old enough to walk on its own. Female gorillas form a strong bond with their babies and stay with them for four years or more before giving birth again.

Gorilla food

Gorillas prefer leaves and stems to fruits. Sometimes gorillas eat ants as well as an occasional worm or grub. Mountain gorillas feed almost entirely on giant celery, nettles, and vines. A mountain gorilla has to eat a lot of leaves because they are low in nutrients.

Amazing facts

- A fully grown mountain gorilla eats 59 lbs (27 kg) of vegetation a day.
- An older male is called a silverback because of the saddle-shaped patch of silver fur on its back.
- The mountain gorilla is the most endangered species of gorilla. Barely 350 of the animals remain in the mountains of Rwanda, Uganda, and Zaire.

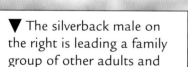

▼ The silverback male on the right is leading a family group of other adults and youngsters.

31

Even-toed Hoofed Mammals

The most common large herbivore mammals belong to the order Artiodactyla. The word *Artiodactyla* means "even toes." Artiodactyls usually have two large toes that form a hoof on each leg and two shorter toes on either side that do not touch the ground. Sometimes these smaller toes are absent. The bones in the foot are long and the ankle is located high up the leg, approximately where human knees are found. With fewer toes and longer legs than other mammals, artiodactyls can run fast to escape predators such as lions and wolves. Although most artiodactyls move very quickly, hippos are slow.

▼ Reindeer have two large toes. Two shorter toes can be seen sticking out behind the hoof.

Feeding habits

Most artiodactyls are either browsers or grazers. Browsers feed on the leaves of trees and shrubs using their narrow muzzles to pick off leaves. Grazers, such as pigs and peccaries, feed on grasses. They root around in the ground using their long snouts and jaw muscles.

▼ Millions of artiodactyls are found on the savanna grasslands of southern Africa. Most live in groups or herds for safety.

These two male antelopes called springboks are fighting over females. They face each other head down, lock their antlers, and push against each other.

Classification key

SUBCLASS	Eutheria
ORDER	**Artiodactyla**
FAMILIES	10
SPECIES	220

Amazing facts

- At about 10 ft (2 m) tall, the giraffe is the tallest animal. The giraffe has an incredibly long neck, but like most other mammals it has only seven neck bones or vertebrae.
- The okapi has a long, black tongue that can curl around leaves and branches to pull them into its mouth.
- The musk ox is named after the strong smell males give off during the mating season. The males fight over the females by charging at each other with their heads down.

Most of these mammals are ruminants—animals that have stomachs with either three or four chambers. The food goes into the first chamber, called the rumen, which contains millions of bacteria that help to digest the food. Then the animal regurgitates the food back into its mouth, creating cud, which it chews again. This softens and breaks up the food so it is digested more easily. Pigs and peccaries are omnivorous. They have a mixed diet and do not ruminate.

Horns and antlers

Many artiodactyls have horns or antlers. Horns are bony outgrowths of the skull covered with either keratin or skin. Most male deer have antlers rather than horns. Antlers are made of dead bone, and they drop off at the end of each year and grow back the following year.

Odd-toed Hoofed Mammals

Odd-toed hoofed mammals are very similar to artiodactyls, except that they have an odd number of toes. The order is called Perissodactyla, and it includes horses, zebras, rhinos, and tapirs. Horses and zebras have a single large toe, while rhinos and tapirs have three toes.

▲ Zebras live on open grassland in scattered herds that can contain hundreds of individuals.

Ancient horses

About 50 million years ago, a small herbivore with three toes walked on the North American grasslands. It was hunted by huge, wolflike dogs and saber-toothed cats, so it relied on speed to escape. This animal was the ancestor of the horse. Slowly, its middle toe became longer and wider, eventually forming a hoof. The legs got longer, too. Longer legs gave it a longer stride so that it could run faster than it ancestors could. In time, the animal took on the appearance of the modern horse. Donkeys and zebras then evolved from the horse.

Classification key

SUBCLASS	Eutheria
ORDER	**Perissodactyla**
FAMILIES	3 (Equidae, Tapiridae, Rhinoceroridae)
SPECIES	78

▼ The tapir has a piglike body with a long head and thick snout.

Feeding

The perissodactyls are not ruminants. Most of the digestion of their food takes place in the rear stomach chamber. This chamber is filled with millions of bacteria that help digest plant food. The food does not stay in the stomach for very long, so perissodactyls can eat large quantities of food each day. They can also survive on poorer-quality grass than artiodactyls.

Tapirs are forest dwellers. They browse on leaves and a variety of fruits and nuts that they find on the forest floor. Tapirs use their incisors to snip off leaves. They use ridged molars to grind up the leaves.

White and black rhinos look very similar even though their names suggest that they have different-colored skin. The white rhino's name comes from the Afrikaans word *weit*, which means "wide." This refers to the animal's wide mouth used to graze on grass. Black rhinos have a pointed upper lip that is ideal for browsing.

Amazing facts

- The zebra's stripes were once thought to be for camouflage, but today most biologists think the stripes help zebras recognize and stay close to each other.
- One extinct species of rhinoceros, Indricotherium, was the largest land mammal that ever lived. It was about 18 ft (5.4 m) tall at the shoulder and weighed around 66,00 lbs (30,000 kg). This is five times the weight of an elephant!
- Rhinos have the thickest skin of any land mammal. The skin on their backs and sides can be 1 inch (2.5 cm) thick.

▼ The white rhino has poor eyesight and relies on its sense of smell to find its way around.

Elephants, Hyraxes, Aardvarks, and Rabbits

There are a number of mammalian orders that contain only a few species and in one case, just a single species. Aardvarks, elephants, and hyraxes are closely related to the even- and odd-toed mammals, while rabbits are related to rodents. All of these mammals are herbivores.

Amazing facts

- An elephant's tusks grow throughout its life and can reach lengths of 11.5 ft (3.5 m).
- Despite their size, elephants can walk silently through the savanna and hardly leave any tracks.
- An elephant's skin is very sensitive. Elephants needs frequent baths and powdering with dust to keep their skin free from parasites and disease.

Classification key

SUBCLASS	Eutheria
ORDER	**Proboscidea**
SPECIES	3

Elephants (Proboscidea)

There are three elephant species: African elephants, African forest elephants, and Asian elephants. The African elephant, which stands up to 13 feet (4 m) high, is the largest living land animal. Females normally weigh up to 4 tons (3 metric tons) and males weigh up to 7 tons (6 metric) tons. Elephants have long trunks that are an extension of their upper lip and nose. Elephants use their trunks to pull leaves from trees and to throw water and dust over themselves. Elephants have large upper incisors called tusks. Their thick, wrinkled skin has little hair.

▼ Elephants use their trunks to drink and throw water over themselves.

Hyraxes (Hyracoidea)

Hyraxes are small mammals closely related to elephants. They are found in central and southern Africa and in parts of the Middle East. The pads of their feet are sticky, and this helps them to climb rocks and trees. The rock hyrax lives in rocky outcrops, while the tree hyrax lives among trees and shrubs. These mammals are considered survivors because they can eat the toughest of plants and survive on very little water.

Classification key

SUBCLASS	Eutheria
ORDER	**Hyracoidea**
SPECIES	11

Aardvarks (Tubulidentata)

The aardvark is an African mammal with a long nose, large ears, and a piglike body. It uses its excellent sense of smell and hearing to find termites and ants. It uses its long, sticky tongue to lick up the insects.

Classification key

SUBCLASS	Eutheria
ORDER	**Tubulidentata**
SPECIES	1

▼ The aardvark has long ears for hearing and a large snout for sniffing out ants, its favorite food.

Rabbits, hares, and pikas (Lagomorpha)

Rabbits, hares, and pikas are found across the world. Like rodents, they have a pair of large incisors, but they have a second pair, too, just behind the upper incisors. These are called peg teeth. The lagomorphs are grazing mammals that spend much of the day feeding on a variety of plants. Rabbits and hares have long back legs that allow them to run fast. Hares can reach speeds of up to 35 miles (56 kilometers) per hour.

▼ The winter coat of the Arctic hare is white to blend in with the snow. Its long ears have black tips.

Classification key

SUBCLASS	Eutheria
ORDER	**Lagomorpha**
SPECIES	58

Rodents

Rodents are small mammals that often have long tails, clawed feet, and chisel-like teeth for gnawing. Rodents are among the most widespread orders of mammals. They are found all over the world, with the exception of Antarctica. Many rodents have moved into towns and cities where they feed on food waste and live in our buildings and sewers.

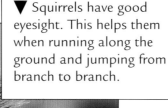

▼ Squirrels have good eyesight. This helps them when running along the ground and jumping from branch to branch.

Chisel teeth

Rodents have pairs of razor-sharp incisors that in many species are tough enough to gnaw through wood. They do not have canine teeth, but they have premolars and molars for grinding food. Gnawing through tough plants can dull rodents' teeth, so their incisors are self-sharpening. A rodent's top and bottom incisors grind against each other, sharpening the teeth into a cutting edge. Their incisors and cheek teeth continue to grow from the bottom throughout their life. This is essential because their teeth are continually worn away.

Classification key

SUBCLASS	Eutheria
ORDER	**Rodentia**
SUBORDERS	3 (Sciuromorpha, squirrel-like; Myomorpha, mouselike; and Caviomorpha, cavylike)
FAMILIES	30
SPECIES	1702

Amazing facts

- Not all rodents are small. The capybara from South America weighs up to 145 lbs (66 kg).
- Beavers are extreme gnawers that can chisel their way through whole tree trunks to build dams. They use logs to build lodges with underground openings.
- Rats are responsible for the spread of disease. Between 1347 and 1350, one in every three people in Europe died from the Black Death, or bubonic plague. It was spread by rats carrying fleas infected with the disease.

Fast breeders

Rodents breed quickly and can give birth to several large litters each year, so their numbers increase rapidly. Around the world, huge numbers of rats and mice destroy crops, invade grain supplies, and carry disease.

▲ A female rat can mate when she is just two months old and can give birth to as many as eleven young.

Squirrels, mice, and cavies

Almost 40 percent of all mammals are rodents. This large order is split into three suborders—squirrel-like rodents, mouselike rodents,and cavylike rodents. This grouping is based on the arrangement of the animals' jaw muscles, which means that each group has a slightly different type of bite. Squirrel-like rodents, such as beavers, marmots, and prairie dogs, tend to have long, slim bodies and hairy tails that they use for balance. Mouselike rodents, such as hamsters, rats, voles, and lemmings, are generally small with pointed faces and long whiskers. Cavylike rodents, such as guinea pigs, porcupines, and chinchillas, are generally larger than the other rodents, with large heads and sturdy bodies.

▼ The porcupine has long spines along its back. When attacked, it raises its spines and charges backward at a predator.

Insect Eaters

The insect eaters, which belong to the order Insectivora, are small, nocturnal mammals with well-developed senses they use to find prey. Although they are called insectivores or "insect eaters," they eat other small invertebrates such as worms and slugs. Most insectivores live on land, but some, such as the web-footed tenrec, have adapted to living near water.

Long snouts

Insectivores tend to have small faces with beady eyes. Their most noticeable feature is a long, slim snout that they use to find prey. The weird-looking solenodon has a particularly long snout that is very flexible and can be pushed into cracks to find prey. Insectivores have small but sharp teeth, and each foot has five clawed toes. Most insectivores live alone, and they are found all over the world except for Australia and New Zealand.

Some insectivores have unusual features. For example, hedgehogs and tenrecs have spines for protection. Moles have large front paws for digging, while solenodons and some shrews produce poisonous saliva.

▲ The desman has a snout that is elongated into a kind of snorkel so that it can breathe while under water.

▼ The European mole spends its life underground. It digs a network of tunnels using its shovel-like front feet, only occasionally popping up to the surface.

Classification key

SUBCLASS	Eutheria
ORDER	**Insectivora**
FAMILIES	6
SPECIES	365

Amazing facts

- The pygmy white-toothed shrew is the world's smallest land mammal. Even when fully grown, it can sit in a teaspoon!

- The star-nosed mole is a strange-looking insectivore. It has a pink, fleshy star attached to the tip of its nose. The animal can use this to find and identify up to five different invertebrates in less than one second.

- Young shrews are led around by their mother in a long chain, each holding on to the shrew in front. This is called a caravan.

▲ Although they are small, shrews can be quite aggressive. They tackle large prey, such as earthworms.

Tiny shrews

There are 300 different species of shrew, and most are smaller than a mouse. Because of their small size, shrews lose heat very quickly, so they have to eat constantly in order to stay warm. Some eat as much as three times their own body weight each day! Many shrews live among fallen leaves on the ground where it is quite dark, and they rely on their sense of touch and smell to find food. Shrews also use sound to find their way around, making high-pitched squeaks and listening to the echoes that bounce off objects.

Cetaceans

Cetaceans, which include whales and dolphins, are mammals that have adapted to an aquatic lifestyle, even giving birth in water.

Streamlined shape

Cetaceans have torpedo-shaped bodies that are wide in front and gradually become narrower toward the tail. Unlike other mammals, cetaceans have no hair, so the surface of their skin is very smooth. Their front limbs are flippers, and they have no hind limbs. Their tails have a unique shape with two horizontal extensions called flukes. The flukes force the animal through the water and provide tremendous swimming power.

▲ When a whale breathes out, a column of warm air and water is forced out of the blowhole on the top of its head. This adult blue whale and its calf are shown from above.

Amazing facts

- The blue whale is the largest animal. It is about 85 feet (26 meters) long and weighs up to 165 tons, as much as 33 of the largest elephants.
- In in the Southern Ocean from 1930 to 1931, more than 31,000 blue whales were hunted by European whalers. Today the population is just 6,000.
- The sperm whale can dive to depths of 3,300 feet (1000 meters) and can stay under water for as long as 90 minutes.

Breathing air

Fish breathe under water using gills, but cetaceans have lungs. Cetaceans have to swim to the surface of the water to breathe air. However, cetaceans can stay underwater for 20 to 30 minutes or even longer. They make each breath of air last much longer by slowing down the rate at which their hearts beat. When swimming at great depths, cetaceans can completely squash their lungs to absorb every bit of available oxygen.

Classification key

SUBCLASS	Eutheria
ORDER	**Cetacea**
SUBORDERS	2 (Mysticeti, or baleen whales, and Odontoceti, or toothed whales)
FAMILIES	9
SPECIES	76

Baleen and toothed whales

The cetaceans are divided into two suborders, baleen whales (Mysticeti) and toothed whales (Odontoceti). Baleen whales are the giant whales such as the humpback, blue, and gray whales. They are filter feeders. Their name comes from the huge baleen plates in their mouths that filter out food from the water. Baleen whales swallow a large mouthful of water that is forced through the baleen plates, trapping food such as plankton, krill, and even fish. On the other hand, toothed whales, such as dolphins, porpoises, killer whales, white whales, sperm whales, and beaked whales, have teeth. They each have a fluid-filled bump on the forehead (called a melon) with a beak in front of it. The toothed whales are hunters, feeding mostly on fish and squid. The killer whale, or orca, even hunts other whales.

▶ The killer whale, or orca, has a powerful tail to propel it through the water. Its tall dorsal fin provides balance.

▲ Dolphins leap out of water when they are being playful, but they also do this to attract other dolphins when they have found a school of fish to eat.

The Humpback Whale

The humpback whale is a baleen whale. It grows to 52 feet (16 meters) long and weighs up to 71 tons. Humpback whales feed on small, shrimplike crustaceans called krill and on small fish. They do not have any teeth. Instead they have up to 400 fringed baleen plates that hang from the upper jaw. During feeding, the grooves in the whale's throat expand so it can swallow a huge mouthful of water and food. When the mouth closes, water is forced out through the plates. The whale swallows the food trapped inside.

A humpback's year

Humpback whales spend the months of June to October feeding in cold waters of the Arctic and Southern oceans where food is plentiful. Then the whales migrate to warmer waters in November, where they stay until February. There they give birth to their calves. They return to cold waters with their calves between March and June. The calves are fed milk that is rich in fat until they are one year old. This helps the calf build up a thick layer of blubber that will enable it to survive in cold water.

▲ These whales are feeding. They take in large mouthfuls of food and water, and filter it through their baleen plates. T baleen looks pink area in this photo.

The song of the humpback

Male humpbacks are famous for the sounds they make. These sounds are called songs. Each song is made up of different sounds, such as snores, groans, ees, oohs, and chirps. A whale song can last up to 35 minutes and forms part of a song session that may go on all day and night. Each individual's song changes over time as new parts are added or removed. No one is sure of the purpose of the whale song, whether it is to attract females or to communicate with other whales.

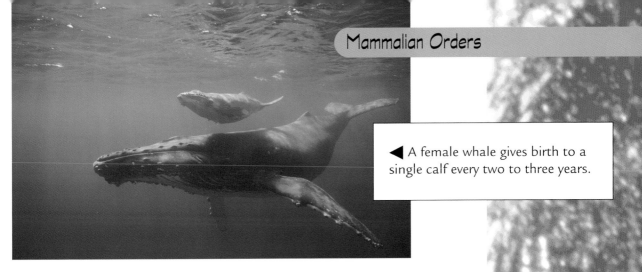

◀ A female whale gives birth to a single calf every two to three years.

Whaling

Humpback whales are slow swimmers whose migration routes take them close to shore. Historically, this made the humpbacks easy to hunt. Between 1905 and 1965, whalers killed about 28,000 humpback whales. In 1966 the whales came under the protection of The International Whaling Commission (IWC). Today, there are about 20,000 humpbacks—one fifth of the population that existed in 1905.

Amazing facts

- The migration of the humpback is one of the longest known in the animal kingdom. The whales of the northern Pacific swim from southeastern Alaska to Hawaii and back each year, a distance of 5,800 miles (9,400 kilometers).

- A humpback whale calf is between 9 and 14.5 feet (3 and 4.5 meters) long at birth and weighs about 1,980 pounds (900 kilograms).

- Each whale eats up to 2,970 pounds (1,350 kilograms) of food a day.

Classification key

SUBCLASS	Eutheria
ORDER	Cetacea
SUBORDERS	Mysticeti
FAMILY	Balaenidae
GENUS	*Megaptera*
SPECIES	***Megaptera novaeangliae***

◀ Humpback whales can throw themselves completely out of the water. This is called breaching.

45

Seals, Sea Lions, and Sea Cows

▲ This Galapagos sea lion is chasing a puffer fish. Sea lions and fur seals have an external ear.

Classification key

SUBCLASS	Eutheria
ORDER	**Pinnipedia**
SPECIES	33
ORDER	**Sirenia**
SPECIES	4

Whales and dolphins are not the only marine mammals. There are two other orders of marine mammals: seals and sea lions (Pinnipedia) and sea cows (Sirenia).

Seals and sea lions

The pinnipeds include seals, sea lions, and walruses. Their name comes from two Latin words that mean "wing-footed." The pinnipeds have adapted to life in water. They have streamlined bodies with powerful flippers and can stay under water for up to 60 minutes. However, pinnipeds return to land to give birth. Seals and sea lions are covered in hair while the walrus is hairless. Pinnipeds are meat eaters, and for this reason many biologists think that they should be classified with the carnivores.

The pinnipeds are divided into three families: the true seals, the eared seals, and the walruses. True seals have no external ear flaps and have sleek fur. Their back flippers point backward. True seals are particularly clumsy on land because they cannot raise their bodies up onto their front flippers. Eared seals include sea lions and fur seals. They have small external ears. Eared seals are far more agile on land because their front flippers can lift the upper body off of the ground. The back flippers can be twisted to lie under the body and can be used to push the animal forward. The most characteristic feature of the walrus is its long pair of white tusks. Walruses have stout bodies with a thick layer of blubber. This helps them to survive in the cold waters of their Arctic habitat.

▲ True seals, such as this northern elephant seal, do not have external ears. While clumsy on land, they are very graceful in the water.

Amazing facts

- When the walrus gets too hot, the blood vessels in its skin enlarge, giving the animal a brick-red appearance.
- The largest pinniped is the southern elephant seal. The male seals can weigh as much as 7,700 pounds (3,500 kilograms).

▲ Manatees, or sea cows, live in shallow water and swim slowly along the bottom in search of food.

Dugongs and manatees

Dugongs and manatees are large mammals that resemble seals. They are often called sea cows. These aquatic mammals live in warm, shallow waters, where they come up to the surface to breathe every 20 minutes or so. They have fat and hairless bodies that measure between 8 and 13 feet (2.5 and 4 meters) long. Their front limbs are like paddles, but they have no hind limbs. Shovel-like tails push them through the water. Manatees are found in the swamps of the Amazon, Florida, and the Caribbean. The dugong is found in the Southwest Pacific and Indian oceans. Dugongs and manatees feed mainly on plants.

The Minor Orders

The orders of mammals covered on this page are less well known than the others, and they contain some very strange-looking animals.

Flying lemurs (Order Dermoptera)

Flying lemurs are mammals that look somewhat like bats. Their names are misleading because they are not lemurs and they cannot truly fly. Rather, they glide from tree to tree using skin that stretches between their neck, fingers, and toes. Flying lemurs live in the forests of Southeast Asia.

Classification key	
SUBCLASS	Eutheria
ORDER	**Dermoptera**
SPECIES	2

Elephant shrews (Order Macroscelidea)

Elephant shrews get their name from their long, pointed snouts. They have a pair of long, powerful back legs for running. They are found in east Africa on grasslands, in forests, and among rocky outcrops.

Classification key	
SUBCLASS	Eutheria
ORDER	**Macroscelidea**
SPECIES	15

Tree shrews (Order Scandentia)

Tree shrews are small, squirrel-like mammals. Despite their name, they live on the ground—not in trees. They have thick, bushy tails and sharp claws. Tree shrews have no whiskers and use their senses of hearing, smell, and sight to find prey in the rain forests of Southeast Asia.

Classification key	
SUBCLASS	Eutheria
ORDER	**Scandentia**
SPECIES	18

◀ Tree shrews have pointed snouts and large eyes.

▲ Many animals, including mites and insects, live in the sloth's thick fur coat.

▲ The giant anteater has a small face with a long snout and long, powerful claws for ripping open termite mounds.

Anteaters, sloths, and armadillos (Order Xenarthra)

These mammals are grouped together because they have unusual joints in their backbones, a relatively small brain, and few, if any, teeth. Armadillos and anteaters are insectivores, feeding on ants and termites. Anteaters have a long, tubular nose and long claws. Their bodies are covered in thick hair. The armadillo has an armorlike covering of hardened skin. Sloths are herbivores and eat leaves and fruits. The sloth spends its life in the trees and uses its long, curved claws to hang from branches. Sloths move very, very slowly.

Pangolins (Order Pholidota)

The pangolin has an armorlike body covering similar to the armadillo, but the covering is made of horny scales rather than skin. Pangolins have no teeth, and long, sticky tongues ideal for licking up ants and termites. A pangolin rolls into a ball when threatened.

Bats (Order Chiroptera)

Bats are the only mammals that have true flapping wings and the ability to fly rather than glide. The wings extend from the legs and sides of the body to the arms, held out by four slender fingers. The knee and foot bend in the opposite direction from other mammals. There are two types of bats: the small insect eaters and the larger fruit bats.

Marsupials

Marsupials are mammals that raise their young inside a pouch on their bodies. They include kangaroos, koalas, and opossums. There are almost 300 different marsupial species, and most of them live in Australia and South America.

Classification key

SUBCLASS	Theria
ORDER	**Marsupialia**
FAMILIES	18
SPECIES	292

Pouched mammals

The most noticeable difference between marsupials and other mammals is the way they reproduce. Marsupials' young are born at a very early stage of development. The tiny young then make an amazing journey, crawling through their mother's fur to reach her pouch. In placental mammals, the young remain inside their mother's body for much longer and are born at a more advanced stage.

▼ This baby kangaroo is attached to its mother's pouch.

◀ A kangaroo baby, called a joey, will leave its mother's pouch to explore its surroundings. However, it hops back in if there is any danger.

▲ The koala is a specialized climber with short, muscular legs and feet that can grip tree trunks. Koalas feed almost entirely on the leaves of gum trees.

Most marsupials have a pouch, a fold of skin on the front of the female's abdomen. In koalas the pouch is a simple fold, while kangaroos and wallabies have a deep, pocketlike pouch. The teats are found inside the pouch, so the young animal does not have to leave the safety of the pouch ... reaches the pouch, it grabs onto a teat ... onths until it is able to open its mouth ... nimal may leave the pouch, but it ... onths. A young red kangaroo spends ... It is fully independent of its mother by

examples of herbivores, omnivores, and carnivores. There is a marsupial mole, a nectar eating honey possum, and a wombat, which is the size of a badger. At one time there was even a marsupial wolf called the thylacine, but it is now extinct.

Amazing facts

- About 50,000 years ago, there were giant kangaroos that stood almost 10 feet (3 meters) high and browsed on trees.

- The saying *playing possum* comes from the habit of the Virginia possum. When faced with danger, this animal lies motionless on the ground for several hours, pretending to be dead. Later, it will get up and run away.

Monotremes

Of all of the mammals alive today, the most primitive are the monotremes. These are egg-laying mammals. There are five species of monotremes, which are found only in Australia and New Guinea.

Egg laying is not the montremes' only unusual feature. The monotremes do not have teeth. Instead,they have a beaklike mouth. Monotremes grind their food between plates or spines in their mouths. Female monotremes feed their young milk, just like other mammals, but they do not have teats. Their milk oozes from glands under a patch of fur on the chest.

▲ The short-beaked echidna has a curved snout and long spines. It uses its sense of smell to find ants and termites.

Echidnas

Echidnas look like fat hedgehogs with small, hairy faces, beady eyes, and long, pointed noses. They have curved claws to rip open the nests of termites and ants. The echidna's body temperature is just 89.6° F (32° C), below that of human beings. Echidnas manage to generate just enough body heat to stay alive.

▼ The long-beaked echidna is covered with fur and short spines. It has short legs and powerful claws.

Classification key

SUBCLASS	Prototheria
ORDER	**Monotremata**
FAMILIES	2
SPECIES	5

The echidna has a strange courtship ritual. The female produces a strong smell that attracts males. Several males follow the female around for up to four weeks. They dig a trench in the ground and then start fighting. The male echidnas butt heads with each other until one male remains in the trench. This echidna will mate with the female. Four weeks later, the female lays a small, leathery egg the size of a grape. The egg sticks to a patch of hair in the echidna's simple front pouch and stays there until the baby hatches ten days later.

The platypus

The platypus looks like a cross between a bird and a mammal. It has a furry body, a ducklike beak, and webbed feet. The platypus' thick covering of fur keeps it warm in water. It shuts its eyes while underwater and uses its beak to find shrimp and mollusks on the riverbed. The platypus stores the food in a cheek pouch before returning to its burrow to eat. A female platypus does not have a pouch. She lays two eggs and then wraps herself around the eggs to keep them warm. About eleven days later, the eggs hatch.

Amazing platypus facts

- A platypus can collect half its body weight in food during a single night.
- Male platypuses have spurs on their back legs that release a poison.

▼ The platypus has a slim body that ends in a flat, fur-covered tail. The webbed feet act as paddles.

Conservation

Around the world, mammals are under threat. Well-known mammals, such as the tiger and gorilla, may become extinct in the wild during the next 10 years. With more than 40 species in danger of extinction, primates are under the greatest threat. The main threat comes from the clearing of forests and other habitats by human beings. Tropical rain forests are home to a huge range of plants and animals, but this habitat is disappearing at an increasing rate. The trees are cut down for timber or fuel wood, or to make way for new farmland, roads, or industry. As a result, animals lose their homes. Most primates live in tropical forests, so it is not surprising that rain forest destruction is putting them at risk.

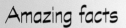

Amazing facts

- Since people started keeping records, 86 mammal species and 24 mammal subspecies have become extinct.
- The International Union for the Conservation of Nature and Natural Resources (IUCN) publishes a list of threatened species. More than 25 percent of all living mammals are on this list.

▼ The snow leopard has pale gray and white fur that was highly prized by the fur trade. Today only a few hundred snow leopards survive in the mountains of central Asia.

Hunting and whaling

Hunting is also a major threat to mammals. For many years, big cats such as tigers and leopards were hunted for their fur, elephants were killed for their ivory, and rhinos were killed for their horns. Today, tigers are hunted for their bones, which some people believe have medicinal value. In central Africa, primates such as chimpanzees, bonobos, and gorillas are hunted for what is called bush meat. Unfortunately, these primates often carry diseases that people can catch if they eat the meat.

Marine mammals have fared no better than land mammals have. Whales have been hunted close to extinction. Commercial whaling was banned in 1986, and the numbers of marine mammals have started to increase again. Today, however, overfishing threatens whales and dolphins. These mammals rely mostly on fish and krill for food, but as people overfish the oceans, there is less food for other animals.

▲ A leopard skin is among the souvenirs on sale in this east African shop.

▲ Sperm whales were hunted for their oil. When a whale was hauled out of the water, it was stripped of its skin and blubber.

Marsupial decline

Some mammals are under threat because their habitats have been invaded by other mammals. The marsupials in Australia survived for millions of years without competition from other kinds of mammals. When Europeans arrived in Australia more than 200 years ago, they brought mice, rats, cats, and dogs. These mammals spread across Australia and competed with the marsupials for food and space. Many marsupials could not survive and died out. Today, rabbits and mice are overwhelming some parts of Australia.

Protecting Mammals

Many mammals are in danger of extinction, so it is important that people protect them. Around the world, conservation organizations and national governments are working hard to find ways to ensure their survival.

Amazing facts

- There were just 200 golden lion tamarins in the rain forests of Brazil during the 1970s. Conservation of the tamarins' home forests has lead to its recovery. In 2001 the population reached 1,000.
- The Californian gray whale was hunted almost to extinction. Once whaling was banned, the species recovered. Now there are more than 17,000 individuals.
- The Antarctic fur seal was hunted for its fur during the 19th century and only a handful survived. It was given protection and now there are more than 1.5 million of these fur seals living on islands around the Antarctic.

▼ Millions of bison once roamed the North American plains, but they were hunted almost to extinction. Yellowstone National Park is one of the few places where wild herds still survive.

Protecting habitats

It is impossible to protect a species without protecting its habitat. Animals and plants depend on each other, so they all have to be protected. For example, without the forests in which bamboo plants grow, the giant panda cannot survive. One of the most important habitats to conserve is the tropical rain forest. Some countries have established huge national parks to protect what remains of their rain forests. The golden lion tamarin is just one animal that needs a rain forest habitat. Although this monkey breeds well in zoos, it can only be reintroduced to the wild if its habitat still remains.

▲ Giant pandas feed almost entirely on bamboo shoots. The forests in which the bamboo grows are declining and this is threatening the remaining pandas.

Breeding in zoos

Sometimes the only way to save a species from extinction is to keep breeding groups of animals in zoos and wildlife parks. Przewalski's horse survives only in captivity. If this horse had not been kept in zoos it would have become extinct. Père David's deer was saved by captive breeding in deer parks in the United Kingdom. It has recently been reintroduced to its natural habitat in China.

Wildlife tourism

Tourism can benefit wildlife. Many people enjoy watching wildlife and they will pay to go on vacations where they can see wildlife. Local communities around the world are realizing that it is important to protect animals and their habitats. They understand that tourists bring new jobs and money into an area. This money can be used to build schools and hospitals. However, the tourism has to be sustainable. This means the number of tourists has to be controlled. Too many tourists can lead to the destruction of habitats. If the animals disappear, the tourists will stop visiting.

▶ Tourism can help conservation. Without the large mammals, few people would visit parts of Africa. Money from tourism can also help the local people.

Classification

Scientists know of about two million different kinds of animals. With so many species, it is important that they be classified into groups so that they can be described more accurately. The groups show how living organisms are related through evolution and where they belong in the natural world. A scientist identifies an animal by looking at features such as the number of legs or the type of teeth. Animals that share the same characteristics belong to the same species. Scientists place species with similar characteristics in the same genus. The genera are grouped together in families, which in turn are grouped into orders, and orders are grouped into classes. Classes are grouped together in phyla and finally, phyla are grouped into kingdoms. Kingdoms are the largest groups. There are five kingdoms: monerans (bacteria), protists (single-celled organisms), fungi, plants, and animals.

Naming an animal

Each species has a unique Latin name that consists of two words. The first word is the name of the genus to which the organism belongs. The second is the name of its species. For example, the Latin name for lion is *Panthera leo,* and that of the tiger is *Panthera tigris.* These names tell us that these animals are grouped in the same genus but are different species. Many animals are given common names that may vary in different parts of the world. For example, *Alces alces* is called moose in North America and elk in Europe. Sometimes there are very small differences between individuals that belong to the same species. So scientists have created extra divisions called subspecies. To show that an animal belongs to a subspecies, another name is added to the end of the Latin name. For example, the tiger has five subspecies, one of which is the Bengal tiger: *Panthera tigris tigris.*

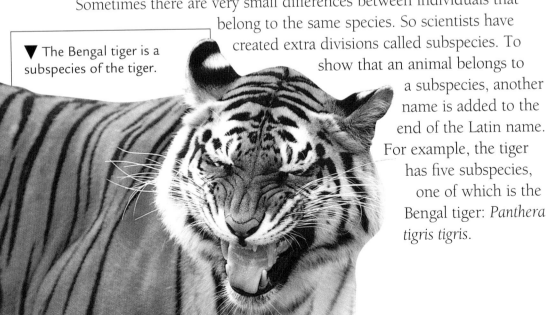

▼ The Bengal tiger is a subspecies of the tiger.

This table shows how a blue whale is classified.

Classification	Example: blue whale	Features
Kingdom	Animalia	Whales belong to the kingdom Animalia because they have many cells, need to eat food, and are formed from a fertilized egg.
Phylum	Chordata	An animal from the phylum Chordata has a strengthening rod called a notocord running down its back.
Subphylum	Vertebrata	Vertebrates have a backbone, a series of small bones running down the back, enclosing the spinal cord. The backbone replaces the notocord.
Class	Mammalia	Mammals provide milk for their young. They are endothermic and usually have a covering of hair.
Subclass	Eutheria (live young)	The whale gives birth to live young. Whales are placental mammals.
Order	Cetacea	Cetaceans are mammals that live completely in water.
Suborder	Mysticeti	Whales of the suborder Mysticeti have baleen plates rather than teeth.
Family	Balaenidae	Members of the family Balaenidae have grooves around their throat that allow them to hold a lot of water.
Genus	*Balaenoptera*	A genus is a group of species that are more closely related to one another than any group in the family. The blue whale's genus is *Balaenoptera*.
Species	*musculus*	A species is a grouping of individuals that interbreed successfully. The blue whale species name is *musculus*.

Mammal Evolution

The origins of mammals date back millions of years. One group of reptiles known as synapsids lived 300 million years ago. These reptiles gave rise to mammal-like reptiles called therapsids. Scientists believe that mammals evolved from this group of reptiles.

▼ The ancestors of elephants first appeared about 60 million years ago.

About 200 million years ago, the first mammals appeared on Earth. They were shrewlike in appearance and just a few inches long. At this time, the world was dominated by giant dinosaurs. The small mammals scuttled around, almost unseen, in the undergrowth of forests. These early mammals had one important advantage over the dinosaurs—they could keep their bodies warm through the night. This meant that they could hunt while the dinosaurs and other reptiles were inactive. However, it was not until 65 million years ago that mammals started to become widespread. A huge meteorite is believed to have crashed into Earth, changing the global climate. The dinosaurs died out and mammals became the dominant land vertebrates.

During the age of the dinosaurs, many different groups of mammals evolved. However, large numbers of mammals became extinct at the end of the last Ice Age. This was a time of major climate change and mammals such as the giant mammoths and saber-toothed tigers disappeared. Today, just three groups remain: monotremes, marsupials, and the placental mammals. The diagram on page 61 shows when the different groups of mammals evolved.

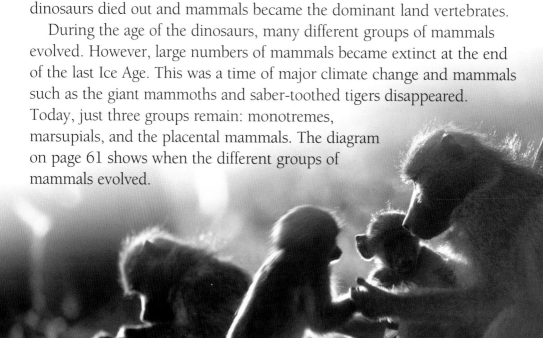

◀ These chacma baboons are placental mammals.

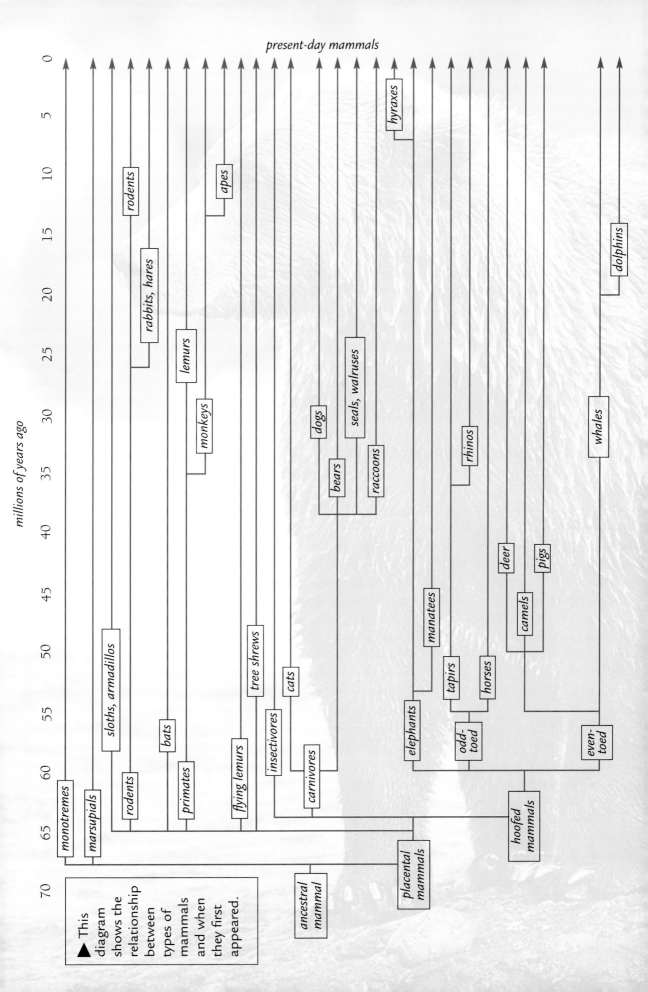

present-day mammals

millions of years ago

0   5   10   15   20   25   30   35   40   45   50   55   60   65   70

▲ This diagram shows the relationship between types of mammals and when they first appeared.

monotremes

marsupials

sloths, armadillos

rodents

rodents

bats

primates

lemurs

monkeys

apes

rabbits, hares

flying lemurs

tree shrews

insectivores

cats

carnivores

dogs

bears

seals, walruses

raccoons

elephants

manatees

hyraxes

tapirs

rhinos

odd-toed

horses

hoofed mammals

camels

deer

pigs

even-toed

whales

dolphins

placental mammals

ancestral mammal

Glossary

abdomen lower part of a mammal's body that contains the stomach, liver, and kidneys

adapt change in order to cope with the environment

blubber thick layer of fat under the skin that helps mammals keep warm. Blubber is found in marine mammals and polar bears.

browse eat leaves from trees or bushes

canine tooth found at the front of the mouth. It is long and pointed in carnivores.

carnivore mammal that hunts other mammals. Cats and dogs are carnivores.

characteristic feature or quality. For an animal, a characteristic would be having hair or having wings.

digit another name for a finger or toe

endothermy having a body temperature that is kept constant regardless of the temperature of the surroundings; also known as warm-blooded

evaporation change in state from liquid to gas, such as when water changes from a liquid to a water vapor

evolution process of change in living organisms so they can adapt to their environment

evolve change very slowly over a long period of time

extinct no longer in existence

fertilize cause a female to produce young through the introduction of male reproductive material

gestation period time it takes from fertilization to the birth of a young animal

gland organ that releases a substance such as saliva or sweat

graze feed mainly on grass

herbivore mammal that eats plants

hibernation deep winter sleep

insulate keep warm

interbreed mate with another animal of the same species

invertebrate animal without a backbone

larva active, immature form of some animals before they develop into their adult form

mammal class of vertebrates that feed their young milk, are usually covered in hair, and have constant body temperatures

mammary gland special gland on a female mammal that produces milk

manipulate handle or use an object in a skillful manner

marsupial pouched mammal. Marsupial babies are born at a very young stage and stay in their mother's pouches until they can move around on their own.

mate act of males fertilizing the eggs of a female of the same species

membrane thin, flexible sheet

migrate regular journey made by an animal, often linked to the changes of the seasons

modified adapted or altered

monotreme egg-laying mammal

omnivore mammal that eats a mixed diet of plants and meat

organism any living thing

placenta area within a mammal's uterus through which food and oxygen pass from the mother's blood into that of the unborn baby

placental having the ability to nurture unborn young through the means of a placenta

poaching hunting animals for their horns, skin, or meat

pouch fold of skin covering teats, found on the front of the abdomen of a female marsupial

predator animal that hunts other animals

prehensile describes the ability to wrap around objects to grip them. Some monkeys have prehensile tails, and elephants' trunks are prehensile.

prey animal that is killed and eaten by other animals

primate mammal that belongs to the order primate. Primates include lemurs, monkeys, apes, and human beings

primitive at an early stage of evolution or development. Monotremes are considered to be primitive mammals because they lay eggs.

regurgitate bring the contents of the stomach back into the mouth in order to chew the food for a second time

ruminant hoofed mammal with a three- or four-chambered stomach that contains bacteria that help to digest grass

saliva fluid produced in the mouth to help an animal chew and digest food

skeleton bony framework of an animal

species group of individuals that share many characteristics and that can interbreed to produce offspring

streamlined describes the slim shape that enables an animal or an object to move easily through water

territory range or area claimed by an animal or group of animals

uterus organ inside a female mammal in which an embryo, or immature young, develops before birth

vertebrate animal that has a backbone

Further Information

Dudley, Karen. *Elephants*. Chicago: Raintree, 1997.

Kinze, Carl Christian. *Marine Mammals of the North Atlantic*. Princeton, N.J.: Princeton University Press, 2003.

Miller-Schroeder, Patricia. *Blue Whales*. Chicago: Raintree, 1998.

Miller-Schroeder, Patricia. *Bottlenose Dolphins*. Chicago: Raintree, 2002.

Miller-Schroeder, Patricia. *Gorillas*. Chicago: Raintree, 1997.

Solway, Andrew. *Classifying Mammals*. Chicago: Heinemann Library, 2003.

Taylor, J.D. *Florida Manatees*. Chicago: Raintree, 2004.

Townsend, John. *Incredible Mammals*. Chicago: Raintree, 2004.

Index